Be The
Master Of
Your Day

6 Simple Strategies to
Manage Your Time &
Boost Your Productivity

AUTHOR: OLIVIA D JOSEPH

www.theoliviajoseph.com

Gratitude

I would firstly start by singing Praises to my Heavenly Father, Almighty God. He has kept me, my family and my loved ones during these trying times.

Covid-19 has caused many to be fearful, become sick, separating families, brought about higher unemployment and high losses in businesses.

I used this to inspire me to write this book.

To my beloved daughters, Sarah and Angel who have been my forever WHY in this life. They are such a blessing to me; they bring me comfort and joy. They are my cornerstone and everything that I am and for that I love them to eternity.

My friend Everald Thompson, who has made me stronger and tougher. Stand up and see everything for what it is. Always look twice to see the real truth. I am grateful for knowing him and learning so much has formed a different way of me viewing life.

v

Mom Gwendolyn , you are the walking breathing rock I stand on your wisdom, wise words and broad shoulders are always there carrying me. I love, appreciate, and value you. SY has left me with so much, imagination, inspiration and motivation, she is smiling on me daily.

	FEB	MAR	APR	MAY	JUN
1	1	1	1	1	1
2	2	2	2	2	2
3	3	3	3	3	3
4	4	4	4	4	4
5	5	5	5	5	5
6	6	6	6	6	6
7	7	7	7	7	7
8	8	8	8	8	8
9	9	9	9	9	9
10	10	10	10	10	10
11	11	11	11	11	11
12	12	12	12	12	12
13	13	13	13	13	13
14	14	14	14	14	14
15	15	15	15	15	15
16	16	16	16	16	16
17	17	17	17	17	17
18	18	18	18	18	18
19	19	19	19	19	19
20	20	20	20	20	20
21	21	21	21	21	21
22	22	22	22	22	22
23	23	23	23	23	23
24	24	24	24	24	24
25	25	25	25	25	25
26	26	26	26	26	26
27	27	27	27	27	27
28	28	28	28	28	28
29			29	29	29
30			30	30	30
31			31		31

www.theoliviajoseph.com

JUL		SEP	OCT		DEC
1	1	1	1	1	1
2	2	2	2	2	2
3	3	3	3	3	3
4	4	4	4	4	4
5	5	5	5	5	5
6	6	6	6	6	6
7	7	7	7	7	7
8	8	8	8	8	8
9	9	9	9	9	9
10	10	10	10	10	10
11	11	11	11	11	11
12	12	12	12	12	12
13	13	13	13	13	13
14	14	14	14	14	14
15	15	15	15	15	15
16	16	16	16	16	16
17	17	17	17	17	17
18	18	18	18	18	18
19	19	19	19	19	19
20	20	20	20	20	20
21	21	21	21	21	21
22	22	22	22	22	22
23	23	23	23	23	23
24	24	24	24	24	24
25	25	25	25	25	25
26	26	26	26	26	26
27	27	27	27	27	27
28	28	28	28	28	28
29	29	29	29	29	29
30	30	30	30	30	30
31	31		31		31

Appendix 1

Bio

Olivia Joseph is an Author, Life/Business Coach, Property Investor/Educator, Professional International Speaker, Chapter Leader for EBW2020 (Sheffield), Philanthropist and CEO of RJ Bell Enterprises.

Olivia as a Life/Business Coach supports ambitious entrepreneurs in the early stages of their business. I ensure they are looking at their business from the fringes when dealing with any challenges they may have along the way. I hold their hand along the journey and make sure stripped of any and all self-limiting beliefs they may have about themselves. I do this to ensure they are confident in the day - to - day running of their life and business.

Olivia works with a wide variety of clients across the continents. Having owned several businesses over the past 20 years Olivia has developed a great understanding of the challenges faced by small and medium size business entrepreneurs.

Olivia's professional background is Law. After several years she left that profession and went into property management and sales. Olivia has always had a passion for real estate.

Olivia's passion is to support and empower women into business globally. She enables women with their business idea to start, grow or scale their business. She assists through mindset changes and tools to get women to be more self- sufficient in their business and only outsource where necessary.

Being born in Georgetown, Guyana I am proud to call Guyana home. Outside of work, I enjoy spending time with my family, cooking, reading and music.

Table of Contents

Introduction

What if you could finally master your time? You would see yourself make more, have more time with your family, and achieve more.

By managing time effectively, you will experience less stress and a better sense of stability in your daily life. Thinking through the details of your day, from the places you work to the routines you implement, will provide a secure structure.

This enables you to let go of thinking about unnecessary details to focus on what is enormously important to you.

These strategies will help you make the most use of your time and be the most productive.

Consider these tools to better manage your time and be more productive:

1. **Chapter 1: Optimizing Productivity with Time and Space.** Visualize your ideal workspace and consider ways to make it a reality. To make the most use of time, think about when the most productivity takes place.

2. **Chapter 2: Focused Task Management.** There are surprising disadvantages to multitasking, context switching, and task switching. Though it may seem impressive to do many tasks at once, you will be more productive if you focus on just one thing at a time.

3. **Chapter 3: Prioritizing Daily Tasks.** How do you decide on the most important tasks? Discover how to get the most out of work time by focusing on the highest-priority tasks.

4. **Chapter 4: Pay Attention to Your Time.** What does it mean to be mindful? If you can focus on the present moment, you will be fully invested in the task at hand.

5. **Chapter 5: Setting Up Your Daily System.** Look at the big picture and then focus-in on the day-to-day reality of making goals come to fruition.

6. **Chapter 6: Set a Schedule, Stick to it.** Consider how you want each hour of your day to flow and create a realistic structure to follow.

Chapter 1: Optimizing Productivity with Time and Space

Using effective time management techniques provides a stability and consistency to daily life. As a result, you will spend less time worrying about the future and more time focusing on the task at hand.

The first thing to consider in mapping out your day is your peak productivity time. Next, think about *where* you are most productive. As you visualize your whole day, you are more able to focus on the small pieces.

Schedule Your Time to Shine

To effectively manage your hour-by-hour and day-by-day routine, you must first ask yourself, *"What is the time of day that I most thrive?"*

Think for a moment about how your most ideal productive day would go. Do you take the morning slow? Do you get right into work? Are you most productive at night?

Once you can pinpoint your most productive hours, you are better able to work out the rest of your day, so you can make the most out of your valuable time.

Perhaps you have found that it is difficult to get productive at all during the day. This frustrating dilemma is one that you can overcome. Though it may be a struggle to get going, once you are in the flow of your work, all will come easily.

Times of Optimal Productivity

- A 2017 California-based research study found that **the most productive time of day is around 11:00 am.**

- **People are most mentally alert between 9:00 am and 11:00 am.** You can use this information while scheduling meetings, as this is the time where people will be the most attentive.

- Information has even been found about the months where people are most productive. **The most productive month of the year is typically October.**

As you walk through the typical layout of your day, picture the parts you might want to change. Perhaps there are daily time management habits that you would like to get rid of. Maybe you have multiple times throughout the day where you find yourself in a productive state.

If you can picture your productivity in 90-minute increments, it might make it easier to place those throughout your day or all in one block.

What if I Only Have a Limited Amount of Time?

Because life is life, there will always be distractions or needs that are unplanned. If you planned to have four hours to work, but you wind up only having one hour, that does not mean the day or the time to be productive must be completely lost. It can be easy to have an all-or-nothing mindset when it comes to following a schedule.

If you cannot do all of it, do some of it.

Once the schedule has been thrown off, it can seem like the rest of the day will be negatively affected as well. This does not need to be the case. To make the most of your time all the time, take the hour you have and do everything you can with it. You do not need to rush.

Choose your highest priority task first. Assign yourself an hour of working on what will move the needle the most, whatever will move you ahead the furthest.

Try these tips to make the most out of a limited amount of time:

- **Take it one minute at a time.** An hour may not seem like a long time. However, a lot of can happen in 10 minutes.

- It can be easy to let an entire hour fly by without having done anything. Minimize distractions. Turn your phone on silent. Focus on exactly what is in front of you.

- **Focus on tasks that will move you the most toward your goal in the time you have.**

- Prioritize the tasks that need the most immediate attention.

The Places That Inspire You

When considering the time of day that you are most productive, you must also consider where you are when you are most productive.

Now, **envision the setting of your ideal, most productive workplace.** Look around. Are there others around you? What does it sound like? Is it a casual or a formal setting?

Perhaps you have a favourite coffee shop where you go to work. Make a regular habit of going to that place at your most productive time of day. If you are not able to get to your ideal setting, create an atmosphere with other qualities that reflect an ideal work setting.

Consider these ideas for places to work:

- **Go to a coffee shop.** Your favourite coffee shop can provide a comfortable and productive familiarity. A coffee shop is a great place to go to get out of isolation and be around people without being directly interrupted.

- **Join a coworking space.** Many cities have coworking spaces. A coworking space has all the amenities of a typical workplace. You can enjoy some great motivation by surrounding yourself with others who are productive.

- **Your office.** If you already work in an office setting, look around the office to see if you can work in your favourite spot. Or, set up your desk to reflect your work needs. If you need minimal distractions, take all distracting items off your desk.

- **Outside.** Refresh yourself and your mind with nature. Find a table in the shade and **take in nature while diving into a productive state**

- **At your house.** If you have a workspace where you live, you can add and remove setting elements according to your ideal environment. Be sure to keep your workspace away from where you sleep. (Save your bedroom just for sleeping!)

-

Who Will You Work With?

Humans are social animals. Some are more social than others. If you find that other people give you energy, consider that fact in choosing where you work. Perhaps you are a social person, but not productive while being social.

Be honest with yourself and **decide based on how you use your time best.** If you have one person or a group of people that you work well around, invite them for a weekly work session and use that time to inspire yourself.

Establishing your best work time and setting will propel you to more effective time management. Asking the simple questions of *when* and *where* will enable you to create the structure that will handle the rest of your day.

Having this environment in place will anchor you to your schedule when obstacles and distractions arise.

.

www.theoliviajoseph.com

Chapter 2: Focused Task Management

While working on three things at time, it can feel like you are getting a lot done. Sometimes a mindset can occur that tells you, *"the more you are doing at once, the more you are getting done."* This thinking is false. In fact, the opposite is true.

When you focus on just one thing at a time, you will achieve higher quality results. Having one thing that you are working on will free up more time. Moving from one thing to another or focusing on many things at once are two ineffective ways to manage time.

You may find yourself beginning a long to-do list, jumping from task to ask. At the end of an hour, you may find that you have attempted many tasks but accomplished none.

There are three obstacles that may come up during your day. All of them can adversely affect time management in different ways. These obstacles are multitasking, task switching, and context switching.

Multitasking

Multitasking involves doing many tasks at once that are all related to the same result. Many people attempt multitasking to be efficient. In fact, it is often celebrated! However, multitasking is not as effective as some believe.

If you think you are an expert multitasker, think again.

For example, you may have experienced walking while trying to type and email on your phone. While these are both tasks that you know well, they become much more difficult when they are done at the same time. This is because your attention is split between two tasks instead of on one.

Task Switching

Task switching is like multitasking in that it involves doing many things at once. However, task switching is even less productive than multitasking. **Task switching occurs while focusing on many things at once that are *not related to one specific goal.***

For example, you may have a conversation on the phone about an upcoming event while writing an outline for a new project. These tasks have nothing to do with each other.

You are more likely to miss important details when you are trying to give your attention to two different things at once.

It can always be difficult to focus. Task switching makes it even harder. The focused feeling of losing track of time and being in the zone is invigorating and productive. This habit prohibits the ability to get totally lost in your work.

Switching from task to task simultaneously means that none of the work produced will be as high in quality as work that is done while only focusing on one thing.

There are two types of task switching: interrupted task switching and rapid task switching.

Interrupted Task Switching

Interrupted task switching occurs most of the time when you have email, social media, and text message notifications.

If you have noise alerts or pop-ups on your computer, you will likely be easily distracted and pulled out of the moment you are having with your work. If you are in a flow state, totally focused and even enjoying yourself, that can all be lost with a simple notification.

An example of this unfortunate interruption is illustrated by our biggest distraction: social media. Once you notice a new social media notification, the moment you click on it you have officially task switched. You may be working on the project in one window while checking social media on the next.

These interruptions are a major obstacle in time management. **They inhibit you from entering the flow state required to get done what you need to.**

Rapid Task Switching

Rapid task switching involves switching from task to task in rapid succession.

Taking notes on your notebook with your computer open to another task is one sure fire way to fall into rapid task switching. You may move from typing an email to writing an outline for a project you are working on in the same second.

Going from task to task in quick succession diminishes awareness not just on your work, but on the rest of the world around you as well. It limits your ability to think clearly and with care.

Context Switching

Context switching occurs when we go from one task to an entirely different task. This is different from multitasking and task switching in that it does not involve doing many tasks at once.

Context switching means moving from one project to another without completing either project.

If you have eight hours in your work time, choose your most important project and work on that. To use your time most effectively, complete that first project before moving on to anything else. If you move from project A before it is done, you will likely end up with two unfinished projects by the end of the day instead of one whole task done.

A huge disadvantage to context switching is that it wastes precious work time. **Once you have come out of focus, it takes about 25 minutes to get into another state of focus**. If you switch contexts three times in your day, you have lost over an hour of time that could have been expertly well spent.

Strategies

Have no fear. Though there are many things that come up, and there is so much to get done with so little time, it is possible to prevent these distracting habits.

Use these strategies to focus on just one thing at a time:

1. **Implement the when and where of your work environment.** When you are in your ideal work setting, you are more likely to become engulfed in your work.

2. **Make it a rule to complete a task before you begin the next one.** This will increase your work endurance and will help you get more done. You will not waste such precious time.

3. **Turn off all your social media and email notifications.** Turn all your technology on *do not disturb* mode. You can even have an auto message letting people know when you will be back online.

4. **Stay away from distracting websites.** You may have a habit of typing in your favourite website when you really meant to check your email. You can avoid this by using applications and reminders that will protect you from distracting websites.

5. **Take advantage of sound.** Put on your favourite background noise or eliminate background noise altogether with noise-cancelling headphones.

Chapter 3: Prioritizing Daily Tasks

Mastering time management does not come easily; it takes practice and consistency.

The best way to ensure that you get done everything on your list is by prioritizing the most important tasks and doing them first.

Prioritization skills come with practice. It may not always be clear what exactly is most important. Though some projects have steps, others are more general and can be accomplished in a variety of ways. Pick out the tasks that are most sure to move you forward.

Ask yourself, "If I complete this task, will I be satisfied with what I have done?" Consider the item that you would do if you could only choose one thing to do. **Which task would move you closer to your goal in the allotted time?**

It can be difficult to know where to start when it comes to prioritizing a to-do list full of important tasks. You can begin the process by talking with others about how they prioritize their work. You can also look at your old habits.

Consider whether your current work habits are sustainable. Do you find yourself with many incomplete tasks during the week? Do you miss deadlines? These might be signs that you need to look at the big picture and re-prioritize your items.

Follow this proven process to prioritize your tasks:

1. **Start by making a list of everything you need to do.** You can make a list that covers the entire week and then break it down in day-by-day sections.

2. **Write any deadlines or time constraints while observing your list.** This will help you determine when you need to start working on what. Be sure to consider the size of each project and deadline.

3. **The night before each workday, look at your list and visualize your day.** What are the tasks that you can get done in your designated work time?

4. **Set aside tasks that are unnecessary or not pertinent to what you are currently trying to get done.** Look at how you want to spend the day and set aside tasks that do not relate to the objectives you have for your day.

5. **It is helpful to start on the most dreadful or difficult task first.** If you first accomplish something that you do not want to do, you will feel less burdened and more motivated.

6. **You can use all these things to set your priorities straight.** Take a step back and weigh the importance of each task according to the goals you have in mind.

Remain Flexible

There are bound to be distractions. New things pop-up, surprises occur, and important phone calls come in. Even though you planned out your day the night before, there are days when nothing goes as planned or things get pushed back.

When these unexpected turns occur, you can use your priorities to guide you towards the tasks to focus on when you do have time. If you have an impending deadline or particularly difficult task, begin with those. If you are asked to take on too much, practice boundaries and avoid promising more than you can deliver.

Use Your Time Wisely

Carefully consider your high-priority items as you look at each day. **Take advantage of your most productive hours by doing the items that need your utmost attention.** Use your time wisely by knowing how things are going to go and giving care to each minute.

www.theoliviajoseph.com

Chapter 4: Pay Attention to Your Time

There are 1,440 minutes in each day. Most people are awake for about 16 hours out of the day. **That means you have about 960 minutes to do what you need to do to have a successful day.** This may seem daunting and it may seem inspiring. Regardless, it is important to be cognizant of the ways you spend your time.

On average, humans can focus for about 20 minutes at a time. However, it is possible to be focused for 20 minutes and then repeatedly refocus.

You can use this information to your advantage when you estimate how long each task will take. If something will take 4 hours, look at it in 20 minute sections. How much of this project can you get done in 20 minutes? How much can you get done in one hour?

Take Planned Breaks

Maintain your attention on each task but be sure to take a break every 90 minutes. If 90 minutes seems like too long, you can also take breaks every 50 minutes. 15 to 20 minutes is a perfect length of time to give your brain a refreshing break.

You can practice being mindful of your time by being mindful during your timed breaks. Practicing a quick mindfulness activity is more effective than taking a break to get on social media or read the news.

Mindfulness enables you to calm your mind and come to the present moment. Social media stimulates the mind and distracts from the present moment.

Try these mindfulness activities during work breaks:

1. **Meditate.** You can meditate for just a few minutes. Sit up straight in your chair. Close your eyes or focus on one point ahead of you. Start to simply pay attention to your breath. Notice, "I am inhaling, I am exhaling."

2. **Go on a walk.** Embrace the feeling of fresh air and sunshine by taking a step away from your work and going on a walk. Leave your phone behind. Simply observe and notice the greenery, the sound of the cars, and the colour of the sky.

3. **Take a colouring break.** Grab a colouring break and set a timer for ten minutes. Use those minutes to relax and colour. This exercise will help keep your mind engaged without thinking about other things.

4. **Notice your five senses.** Take a moment to notice all your senses. What do you hear, see, smell, taste, and feel? Go through all your muscle groups and relax them, starting with your toes and ending with your ears.

Set Reminders: Check Yourself

Set reminders for yourself to help notify you of an upcoming transition in your day. These small alerts can serve as a line of accountability when you are trying to practice new habits.

If you notice a "ding" five minutes before it is time to move on to your next task, you will be able to find a stopping point and make a smooth transition to the next item of business.

You can also take advantage of the opportunity that an alert presents.

Use a small moment in your transition to acknowledge your day and check that your focus is on the task at hand. You do not always have to stop what you are doing to be mindful. You can take advantage of moments at work where you can bring your attention to exactly what you are doing.

If your next task calls for movement, bring your focus to your walking. Feel the ground beneath your shoes and focus on your breath, even if just for a moment.

It is easy to look to the future and concern ourselves with imagined scenarios that we truly cannot predict. **These small moments of mindfulness can provide a chance to let go of worry and focus on the task at hand without disrupting your day.**

How Does Mindfulness Affect Productivity?

An ability to focus on the present moment brings about a stronger connection to the task at hand rather than your entire to-do list. Those who practice mindfulness have been shown to be less affected by distractions.

Mindfulness increases productivity by creating a manageable stream of thoughts that do not overwhelm. By practicing mindfulness regularly, you are likely to increase your ability to regulate emotions. This stability provides focus on only the thoughts that count.

Treat your time with care and attention. The best way to be mindful of your time is to be aware and conscious of what you do and when you do it. You can do this by creating a system, or a routine, for each day.

Chapter 5: Setting Up Your Daily System

Time management is not just about getting stuff done. **Time management is about structure and consistency.**

Structure provides a sense of security and relief to each day. It decreases the need for worry or time-wasting thoughts.

If you already know how the first three hours of your day are going to go, you do not need to wake up and wonder how the next three hours will go. You will already know because you have a system.

Follow a Routine.

Working within a structure, no matter how subtle, provides numerous benefits. **By having a routine, you are more likely to not just be more productive, but also to feel better all around.** You will get sounder sleep, feel less stressed, and have a stronger ability to focus on each task at each designated time of day.

You can begin thinking about your routine by splitting your day into sections.

Begin with the first hour. What does the first hour of your day look like? **Try to spend the first hour of your day *off technology*.** Avoid checking your email or responding to text messages. Take the first hour of your day just for yourself, so you can transition into your day.

By preparing, thinking through, and strategizing for the day ahead, you will feel a greater sense of stability.

Ask yourself these questions about your routine:

1. **Morning Routine**
   - What is the first thing you want to do each morning?

   - What is the second thing you want to do each morning?

   - What will make your morning feel like a success?

   - What is the most important daily task you will do each morning?

2. **Nightly Routine**
   - How do you want to end your day?

   - How will you wind down from your day?

   - What is the most important task you want to do each night?

   - What task will help you feel a sense of completion about your day?

What are the most important things you want to get done in the morning? Accumulate small successes early on in your day. This will help you feel confident and ready for your day.

For example, you can start your day by making your bed. **Though this may seem insignificant, making your bed starts your day in a refreshingly successful way.** It lets you know that you are officially beginning your day, it gives you a success right away and a nicely made bed is waiting for you at the end of each day.

Think about the rest of your day in sections, as well. What do you do before you work? When do you take breaks? When do you eat? Consider these questions as you walk yourself through your day.

Once you have basic routines that take care of the little stuff, look at your long-term goals to come up with a daily system. Create your system based on what's right in front of you. Though you have goals, having a system is a better use of your time and productivity.

What is the Difference Between Goals and Systems?

Goals are important. They motivate us to become the people we are meant to be. They guide us through the storms of life by providing a light at the end of the tunnel. Goals determine our values and the way we live our lives. **We look at the future and the bigger picture of our life in the long-term when we set goals.**

Systems are also important. **Systems zoom in on the day-to-day and minute-to-minute details** on the actions that will bring your long-term goals to fruition.

However, if you spend all your time looking at the goal on the horizon, you might lose track on what is right in front of you. Instead of only focusing on the future, look at this exact moment. Look at each moment and the role it plays in propelling you to success.

To create your system in the most effective way, you must start by setting your goals. Big picture goals are based on the lifestyle and career paths that you want to pursue. Systems are the building blocks to those goals.

Follow this process to set long term goals:

1. **Consider your values.** What do you consider "success?" Do you want to accumulate a fortune? Accolades? Community? Think about what your life will look like when you feel that you have reached your full potential.

2. **Zoom-in on one aspect of your desired outcome.** For example, consider what job you would like to have. What kind of person do you want to be? Five years from now, what would you like to have accomplished?

3. **Time your goals realistically.** Think about how long it might take you to get to your goal. This will help you visualize your goal. Be careful not to take on too much. You want to set yourself up for success instead of disappointment.

Building a System

Once you have a long-term goal set in place, you will be able to set up your day-to-day system. Break down your goal into six-month intervals. Next, break it into one-month intervals. Finally, think about the specific things you need to do on a daily or weekly basis to take constant steps toward the official destination.

Your system consists of the daily things you do and focus on that move you forward toward your long-term goal.

By creating your daily system, you will be able to let go of the future and focus on enjoying the present moment. **You will not need to worry about your goal when you are following your system because success is built into each day.**

For example, imagine you have a goal to write a 300-page book in one year. What do you need to do each day to reach that goal? By breaking down each page into month sections, and taking one day off per week, you could realistically write 500 words per day. So, at what time of day would you write?

Build your system based on your long-term goal. When there is a long-term goal, the small steps support that goal. You do not need to keep your eyes on the prize. **You only need to keep your eyes on this present moment.** By doing this, you will experience less stress and a greater likelihood of success.

The step you take each day to work towards the finish line can be seamlessly placed through each part of your day. Set up the rest of your day to reflect the goals you want to work towards.

www.theoliviajoseph.com

Chapter 6: Set a Schedule, Stick to It

Lay out your entire day by creating a realistic schedule of your day-to-day system. To make the most effective use of your time and be the most productive, **map out the hour-to-hour details that comprise each of your days.**

Before you schedule anything, look at the way you are currently spending your time. **Take one week to observe each hour of your day.** Document the way you currently spend your time. This exercise will help you create a structure that can provide support and help you make the most use of your time with the least amount of stress.

An Example of a Schedule on a Typical Day:

Time	Task
7:00 am - 8:00 am	<ul><li>Wake up</li><li>Make bed</li><li>Meditate</li><li>Eat breakfast</li></ul>
8:00 am - 9.00 am	<ul><li>Go To work</li><li>Review to-do list and priorities</li><li>Check email</li></ul>
9:00am - 12:00 pm	<ul><li>Work on tasks in order of priority</li><li>Take planned breaks at least every 90 minutes</li></ul>

SMART Goal

Initial Goal	Write your goal here.
S Specific	Your goal should be well defined, detailed and clear.
M Measureable	Is your goal measurable? You should be able to tell when you reach your goal.
A Achievable	Can you reach the goal, taking into account your available time, skills and financial status.
R Realistic	Is your goal realistically achievable within the given time frame and with the available resources?
T Timely	Set a start and finish date for your goal. Start Date............................ Finish Date...............................
SMART Goal	Revise your goal based on the questions above.

Action Plan
What steps do you need to take to get you to your goal?

Action Items	Expected Completion Date	Actual Competion Date

Potential Obstacles and Soloutions

Potential Obstacles	Potential Soloutions

Appendix 2

Reduce the Scope!

You do not need to do everything all in one day. **If you put too much on your plate, you will wind up losing more time and producing less work.**

Imagine a doctor who books too many patients in one day. If there is any disturbance in the schedule, the waiting room will grow more crowded as the wait gets longer.

Reduce the scope of your day and focus only on what is realistic. If you end up taking on too much, it will be harder to follow a schedule. A full plate is a catalyst for stress and incomplete work. Be quick, but do not hurry. Avoid overwhelming yourself to be efficient.

Leave No Task Untouched

Maintain the order of your day to the best of your ability. If you have a daily routine you want to follow, stick to it. **Follow the order of each event, even if you no longer have the planned amount of time.**

For example, if you planned to clean your house for an hour, but only have 20 minutes, you can focus on one room and get that done.

This habit will also help you maintain your daily schedule in the long run, even if it does not work on one day. Things may not be going as planned, but time can still be used wisely. Even though not everything was accomplished, the feeling of success will still come after doing everything that you could.

Batching

When you batch your days, your complete tasks that are like each other in sections.

For example, you might have one hour on your schedule to check emails and return phone calls. You can split your days into sections and create a streamlined organization.

There seems to be a culture that encourages constant email-checking. **However, new research suggests checking email just three times per day**. For some, this sounds stressful. The fear of missing out comes into play, which makes checking email irresistible.

This habit is a difficult one to break. You can start small -- check your email five times per day. You can even let people know that all their emails will be responded to within 24 hours.

Social media is a huge part of the daily life of many people. It has become a natural way to communicate and connect with those within our community and throughout the world. Social media can also be as addicting as checking email.

A healthy habit to implement is one of conscious social media time. Rather than checking notifications every time there is a free moment, choose a time of day that you will dedicate to social media.

Batching Categories

Here are some examples of categories that may work well for your time management when you batch them together:

1. **Professional Correspondence**
   - Check email.
   - Return phone calls.

2. **Social Hour**
   - Check text messages.
   - Coordinate social plans.
   - Check social media.

3. **Current Events**
   - Check in on the news.
   - Get updates on topics of interest.

4. **Self-Improvement**
   - Go to the gym.
   - Work towards your long-term goal.

You can examine the rest of your schedule and look at your most productive time of day to choose where you batch which tasks. **Use your productivity time to your advantage and create a schedule according to which tasks need the most attention.**

There are even days of the week when you might want to take care of an entire category of tasks.

Theme Your Days

Some activities do not need to be done every day. For example, you might not need to go to the grocery store every day. Activities that can be put on just one day can be categorized into themes for your days. If you have multiple errands to do each week, choose just one day to do all of them.

These themes are part of your weekly rituals and habits that you want to maintain over time.

Whether you take your dog to the dog park once a week or choose one day each week to have meetings with co-workers, doing them on the same day each week will create a stable consistency.

Consider these suggested themes:

Mastery Mondays
- Practice a new hobby.
- Improve on a new skill.

Productivity Tuesdays
- Complete big projects.
- Schedule meetings for this day.
- Dedicate extra focus to work.

Workout Wednesdays
- Schedule a longer workout session.
- Work with a professional trainer.

Thinking of your weeks in sections like this helps you to focus on the day ahead rather than the month or year ahead.

Make Time for Fun

Create time to pursue the things you love that are not work related. A great way to reward yourself after a satisfying and hard day of work is by engaging in one of your hobbies. Productivity is essential. Embracing hobbies is also an essential way to avoid burnout.

When you have scheduled your day and prioritized your tasks, you will be better able to make time for the things you love. **If you find that you have so much on your plate that you do not have time for fun, the solution is not to eliminate fun.**

Instead, start by carving out as little as an hour per week to dedicate to a hobby. Whether you most enjoy cross-stitching, rock climbing, or juggling, you can make time for both your high priority responsibilities and your extracurricular hobbies.

It can be difficult to find hobbies as life takes over. Time flies by as the hustle and bustle determines how our days go. By taking charge and making positive changes in your time management skills, you will suddenly find that you have more free time to dedicate to fostering a well-rounded lifestyle.

Short on fun? Use these techniques to choose a new hobby:

1. **Make a list.** Write down all the things you are interested in. You do not need to have an end plan in mind, just jot down the first things that come to mind. For example, you may be interested in astrology, painting, and filmmaking.

2. **Once you have a list of interests, choose a couple to try out.** By exploring a new hobby, you will broaden your horizons and have a stronger ability to approach work with a fresh outlook.

3. **Avoid limiting yourself.** You do not have to have just one hobby. You can pursue several things you are interested in. Just ensure that you do not take on too much.

The Bottom Line

Take inventory of your daily life and **let go of the habits that no longer serve you.** Acquiring new time management skills will foster a greater spark of productivity that will endure through the obstacles that naturally arise.

You do not have to expend energy and worry on the organization of your day. Regular practice and implementation of a few simple skills can save you time so that you can better focus on what is pertinent to the current moment.

Follow this process to integrate effective time management skills into your daily routines:

Step 1: Begin by considering when you are most productive. Take stock of what your days currently look like and make realistic adjustments to use your time most effectively

- Use your highest alert times to take care of your highest priority items. Schedule your meetings and free time according to the ebb and flow of your day.

- Create your ideal setting for productivity. **Think about where you feel the most comfortable.** Find an accessible and consistent setting where you can focus and get into the flow of your workday.

Step 2: Choose one task to focus on at a time. Let go of old multitasking habits that halt productivity, diminish work quality, and stir up more stress. Use strategies that will limit distractions. This will help you maintain focus.

- It takes around 25 minutes to refocus on a task once you have broken focus. Switching from task to task is unproductive and will end up wasting time. It is best to focus on each task as it comes.

- **Complete one task before moving on to the next.** A day with one complete project is more successful than a day with two incomplete projects.

Step 3: Examine the importance of each task ahead of you. Depending upon time constraints and level of focus, prioritize your tasks. Begin your work time with the most important task.

- Despite all the planning in the world, many days go in a different direction than intended.

- **Remain flexible in the face of distraction or interruption.** Referring to your prioritized list can help you make decisions about how to use a limited amount of time.

Step 4: Be attentive of your time. Take care to notice how you spend each day. The day does not need to be daunting or overwhelming.

- **Planned mindfulness breaks will help the day go by at an even pace.** Take a step back after around 90 minutes of work time. In doing so, you will be able to maintain a consistent work pace and quality of focus.

- **Follow a simple and consistent routine.** Think of your day in sections. Consider what each part of your day looks like, beginning with the moment you wake up.

Step 5: Develop and sustain an efficient system in which you will thrive. A system is created based on your long-term goals. Instead of constantly looking towards the future, bring your attention to what you can do each day that will inevitably lead to your goals.

- Goals are based on the long-term, big picture ideas for your life.

- Systems are the small, daily steps that lead to achievement of those long-term goals.

Step 6: Create a schedule that works for you. Be careful not to take on more than you can handle.

- **Knowing your limits is good for you, good for your work, and good for the people around you.**

- If your daily schedule is disturbed, do your best to get to every task. If you planned an hour but only have twenty minutes, spend a focused, productive 20-minute period on the scheduled task.

- Categorize sections of your days based on the similarity of different tasks. If you have administrative tasks to do, do them all in the same part of your day.

- Spend less time checking your email. Schedule times to check your email and take care of those responses during planned parts of your day.

- **Pursue hobbies.** Making time for intentional fun ensures a consistent and stress-free quality of life. Though life may sometimes seem too busy for hobbies, you can make time for them when you implement effective time management skills.

A natural consequence of time management is an increase in productivity. Distractions and worries are minimized when your days are predictable and simple. Consistent and regular practice of these time management tools are the catalyst for innovation and growth.

Putting Goals into ACTION

Start Date: _____

Target Date: _____

Completion Date: _____

Goal – Written in the form of a statement. Must be SMART (Specific, Measurable, Agreed Upon, Realistic, Timely)

Specific

Measurable

Agreed Upon

Realistic

Timely

Expected Results (How will you feel when you achieve your goal?)

1.

2.

3.

4

5.

Agree Upon with _____Date_____

Appendix 3

Specific steps to Achieve Goal	Target Date	Completion Date
1.		
2.		
3.		
4.		
5.		
6.		
7.		
8.		
9.		
10.		
11.		
12.		
13.		
14.		
15.		
16.		
17.		
18.		
19.		
20.		

Is this goal in alignment with your values?

Is achieving this goal worth the time and effort involved?

Yes___ No ___

hello 2 0 21!

MY INTENTION + PURPOSE

---

3 THINGS I'D LIKE TO ACCOMPLISH

MY WORD FOR THE YEAR

PEOPLE TO MEET	PLACES TO GO	THINGS TO DO
BOOKS TO READ	RECIPES TO TRY	PROJECTS TO START

Appendix 4

NOTES

www.theoliviajoseph.com

@COACHOJ

Empowering Beliefs to Make You Strive

1. *I* take responsibility. You oversee your life. Hold yourself accountable for the outcomes you create. Celebrate the fact that you have the power to determine your own future.

2. *I* apply effort. Figure out your definition of success so you know what is worth working for. Give yourself credit when you are making progress rather than comparing yourself to others.

3. *I* leverage my strengths. You have your own individual strengths that you can draw on. Figure out what you are good at and what you want to do. Let that knowledge guide your choices.

4. *I* listen to feedback. Ask for feedback so you can enhance your performance and show others that you respect their point of view. You grow faster when you gather solid input that you can translate into action.

5. *I* ask for help. Expand your capabilities by building a sturdy support network. Carpool with other parents. Divide up household chores with your spouse and children.

6. *I* connect with others. Moral support counts too. Surround yourself with loving and encouraging family and friends. Participate actively in your faith community. Join a club with members who share your interest in solar power or badminton.

7. *I* recognize opportunities. Stay alert for promising openings. You may meet a new friend while you are standing in line to buy your morning coffee.

8. *I* try new things. Be open to experimentation. Go kayaking one weekend instead of playing tennis. Bake your own bread or knit a scarf. You may discover hidden talents.

An upbeat attitude increases your happiness and productivity. Question your old assumptions so you can replace them with a new sense of certainty about yourself and your future. Adopt empowering beliefs that build up your confidence and prepare you for greater success.

Start today. You will be glad you did!

NOTES

NOTES

Appendix

www.theoliviajoseph.com

Printed in Great Britain
by Amazon